An Amazing Journey

By Suzanne Weyn

Illustrated By Mary Collier

CELEBRATION PRESS
Pearson Learning Group

Contents

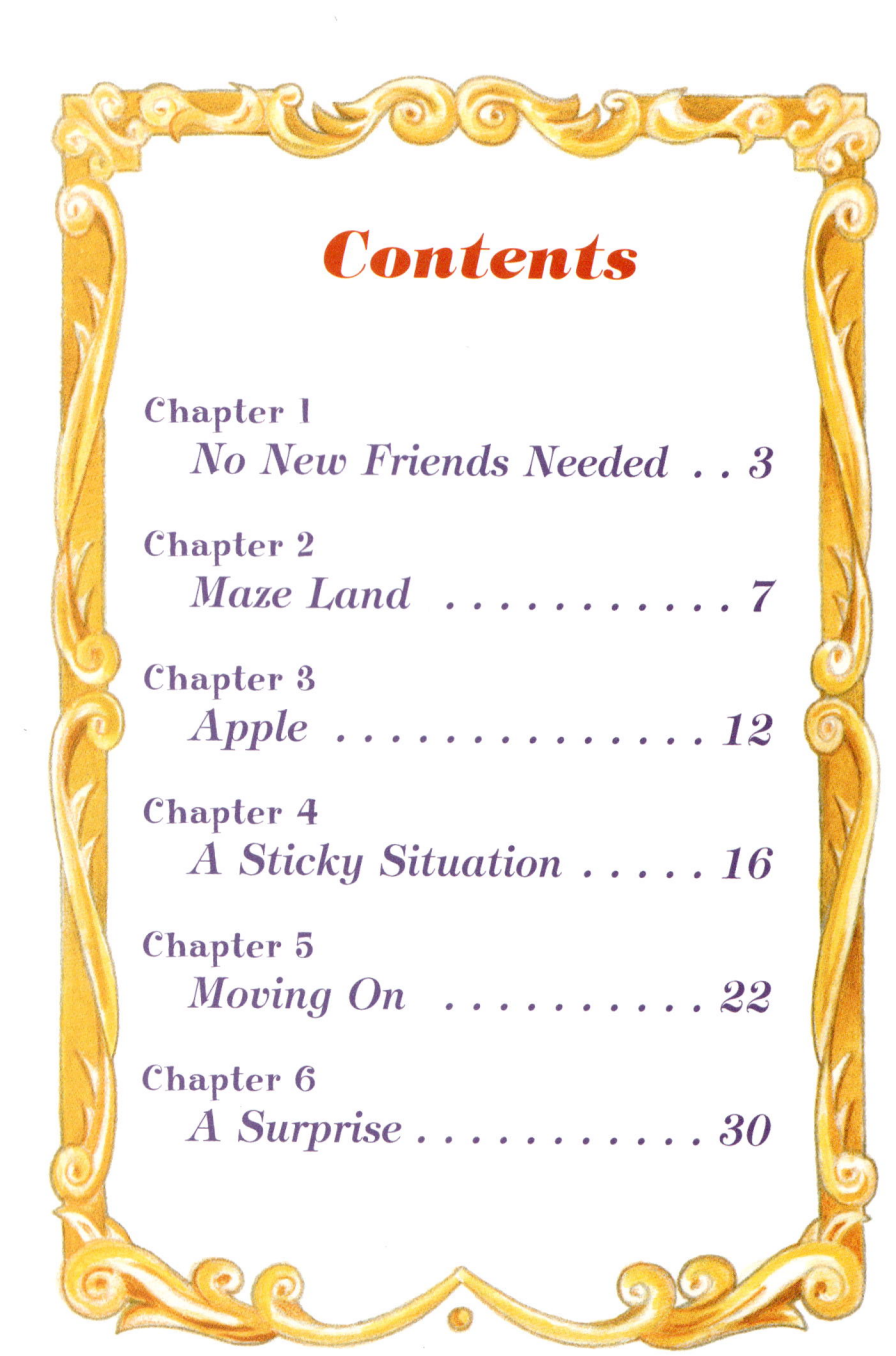

Chapter 1
No New Friends Needed . . 3

Chapter 2
Maze Land 7

Chapter 3
Apple 12

Chapter 4
A Sticky Situation 16

Chapter 5
Moving On 22

Chapter 6
A Surprise 30

Chapter 1

No New Friends Needed

"A family with children is moving in across the street," Emma's mom said as she looked out the window. "It will be terrific having more children in the neighborhood."

Emma looked up from the maze book she was working on and asked, "What? Oh, new kids—that's fabulous." Truthfully, she wasn't really all that interested in meeting them.

Emma knew how moving felt. She and her family had moved in just a few weeks ago. Because of her dad's job, they moved to many places. *There was no point in making new friends,* she thought. She would just have to leave them, and that was too hard.

Emma's mom looked out the window again. "I see a girl around your age. Do you want to walk across the street with me? It might be fun to meet new people."

"Do I have to?" Emma asked.

"Emma, you haven't tried to make friends with anyone," her mom said.

"I don't want friends that I'll just have to leave," Emma said. "It hurts too much."

"Dad says we might not have to move again," her mom reminded her.

Emma did not believe it because something always seemed to happen at her dad's job. Then they had to move again.

"I'd rather work on my mazes," she said. "They're something fun to do alone."

The phone rang, and Emma's mom hurried to answer it. Curious, Emma gazed out the window at the big moving van. Several children were helping adults carry furniture and smaller items into the apartment building. It might be fun to have a friend, but then again, it would be too depressing to leave that friend behind.

With a sigh, Emma continued working on her mazes. She enjoyed the way the paths wound around one another. Sometimes the paths tangled, and sometimes they went in different directions. It was hard to find the right path.

She picked up her pencil and turned to a maze with the title, *An Unusual Maze.* As soon as she touched her pencil to the beginning of the maze, the room began to fade.

Chapter 2

Maze Land

To Emma's absolute surprise, her living room had completely disappeared. She now stood by a faded red barn, at the foot of three roads that stretched out in front of her. A very tall hedge separated each road.

Suddenly, a man in blue overalls strolled out of the barn. Emma called to him, "Excuse me, could you tell me where I am?"

"People around here call this place Maze Land," he said in a slow voice.

"How did *I* get here?" she asked.

He scratched his chin and said, "Well, most people just pop in, like you did."

"Where do these roads lead?" she asked.

"One road leads right back here," he said. "That's the one you want to avoid. One road takes you to a dead end, and the third road takes you wherever you want to go."

"How long have you been here?" Emma asked.

He squinted his eyes and said, "I've lived here for my entire life."

"Really?" Emma asked excitedly. "Then you must know which road I should take."

"Well, I can't help you with that. I've never been much interested in these roads. However, I can tell you that no one should attempt these roads without Apple," he said.

"Who's Apple?" Emma asked.
"She's a girl who walks by here around this time every day," he replied. "She should be coming any minute now, so I suggest that you wait for her."

Emma looked down the road to see if this girl Apple was coming, but she didn't see her. When Emma turned back around to ask the man what Apple looked like, he had vanished!

Emma wasn't about to stay there and wait for some girl she didn't know. She had to find her way out of this strange place and return home. So, looking at the three roads, she decided to take the middle one.

As Emma was walking, she noticed that the ground beneath her was smooth, and on either side of her were hedges that were too tall for her to see over. Colorful birds and butterflies flitted in and out of them. Emma felt pleased with her choice because it seemed so beautiful and peaceful.

Soon, Emma came to something that forced her to stop. In front of her was a cluster of enormous oak trees that were very close together. Their thick branches were so intertwined that they created a tree wall with very little space in between them. Even though it appeared difficult to do, Emma would have to try to get past the trees.

Emma studied the trees carefully. She couldn't see to the other side, but she needed to keep going down the road to find out if it would lead her home. Finally, Emma figured that with some luck, she could slip between the tree trunks if she sucked in her breath and made herself as slender as possible. She was a little afraid, but she was determined to try anyway.

Chapter 3

Apple

Emma took a deep breath, turned sideways, sucked in her stomach, and stepped between two trees. As soon as she did, branches scooped her up and carefully put her back onto the ground. Emma was too startled to speak. Getting up, she faced the trees again, now even more determined to get through them than she had been before.

Emma sprinted forward, threw her arms up to cover her face, and plunged headfirst into the space between the two trees. Again, the branches picked her up and gently deposited her back onto the ground.

This is impossible, Emma thought. "I really need help with this," she said out loud. Suddenly, she saw a spark and smelled something sweet.

Out of nowhere, a girl appeared. The girl's hair was a mass of wild red curls, and when she moved, tiny bells on her ankle bracelets jingled. She wore colorful clothes and no shoes.

"Are you Apple?" Emma asked.

"Yes, I am," Apple replied.

"I'm trying to get home, but I can't get through the trees," Emma said. "A man said that you might be able to help me."

"I can't help you get through those trees because this is a dead end," said Apple.

Emma didn't like the idea of giving up and demanded, "How do you know that?"

"I've been here before. We have to go back and try another road," Apple replied.

"Couldn't we just climb over the hedges?" Emma asked.

"I don't know," Apple said. "I've never tried that, but it sounds like a good idea."

Apple cupped her hands, and Emma stepped into them. Then Apple pulled her hands up and boosted Emma upward.

Emma landed on top of the hedges and cried, "Whoa!" as she tried to balance herself. When she was steady, Emma reached down to pull Apple up, but the girl wasn't there. Emma looked around. *Where had she gone?*

Chapter 4

A Sticky Situation

Now Emma didn't know what to do. Then she heard, "Jump! I'll help you!" from the other side of the hedges. *How had Apple gotten over there?* Emma thought.

Emma didn't think about it for long. She just wanted to get back home. "All right, here I come!" she cried. Shutting her eyes, Emma leaned forward, and down she went.

As Emma got up, she noticed that the hedges were gone, and there were now brick walls on both sides of her. "What happened to the hedges?" she asked.

"In Maze Land, the roads are constantly changing," Apple answered.

I'm glad Apple is with me, Emma thought.

The girls began walking down the new road. The road was straight at first, but soon it twisted to the right over another road.

A little way farther, the two roads started to twist and turn around and around each other. One of the roads wandered off to the right, and one went to the left.

"Does it matter if we stay on the same road?" Emma asked.

Apple nodded and said, "One of these roads leads back to the barn. If we get on that road, we'll wind up back there and have to start over."

Apple explained that the only way to be sure they were still on the right road was to keep turning and twisting carefully along with it. After a while Emma was getting tired, and the turning had made her dizzy.

"I need to rest," Emma said and began walking onto the grass. As she was walking, the grass turned blue, and instantly, Emma realized that she couldn't lift her feet.

Emma tried to yank her foot up, but it was pulled down by some kind of blue goo. "I'm stuck!" she called to Apple.

"I'll save you!" Apple called as she tried to lean over and reach Emma to pull her out. Emma grabbed Apple's hand, but the goo was too sticky, and she ended up pulling Apple in with her.

"Now we're *both* stuck!" Emma cried.

"You're right," Apple said, "but don't worry." She took a book titled *What to Do When Stuck in Blue Goo* from her pocket and began to read.

Emma had the feeling that she was slowly sinking deeper into the goo. Looking at her feet, she saw it was true—she was now sunk down to her knees. "Hurry up!" she said to Apple anxiously.

"The book says to close your eyes and *think* yourself out of the goo," Apple said.

"Is that really what it says?"

"Yes, just do it," replied Apple.

"It's not working," grumbled Emma as she slowly opened one eye.

"You need to try harder," Apple insisted.

Emma squeezed her eyes shut and pictured herself on the road again. When she opened her eyes, she was no longer sinking, and her feet were back on the road—it had actually worked!

Chapter 5

Moving On

Emma looked back to where Apple had been stuck, but Apple wasn't there. *Now, where did she go?* Emma thought.

"I'm right here," Apple replied, as if reading Emma's mind.

Emma quickly turned around, and there was Apple, standing behind her. Emma said, "I'm glad you had that book with you."

"I always carry it with me," Apple said, picking goo from her sleeve. "You never know when you might find yourself stuck in blue goo."

Emma smiled and thought about their situation. She didn't want to end up back at the barn, and the thought of taking one of the roads over and over again was awful. It upset her just to think about it.

Apple studied the roads, then looked over at Emma. "I know what you mean," she said, even though Emma hadn't said anything. "It will be difficult to pick a road, but I have an idea. Stand behind me and put your hand on my shoulder. We'll stay together and take tiny steps."

That sounded like a good plan, so Emma got behind Apple. Together they started moving forward with small steps.

"This is hard to do," Emma complained.

"Pretend it's a game," Apple advised, "and it won't seem so difficult."

After a series of turns, the road they were on untangled from the other road and headed out in a straight line. "We did it!" Apple cheered as she jumped for joy.

"Are you certain we're not heading back to the barn?" Emma asked.

"No, I'm not sure because the roads are different every time I travel on them," said Apple. "I think this is right, but there's only one way to find out. Let's keep going."

Emma hesitated for a moment but decided to trust Apple. She was glad that she was with someone who didn't pretend to know more than she really knew.

The girls kept walking down a road that now had tall buildings on both sides. No one else was around. From time to time, Emma looked at Apple, who whistled a happy tune as they walked. Emma realized it was nice having Apple with her. She knew she would have been much more worried and afraid if she had been alone.

Suddenly, Apple stopped in front of a building and said, "I think this is it."

They entered a building with a high ceiling and a marble floor. An elevator door faced them. "If you take that elevator to the top floor, I think it will take you home," Apple said. "It has worked for other people."

"Aren't you going to come with me?" Emma asked. She had grown to like Apple a lot and didn't want to leave her new friend behind.

Apple shook her head and said, "No, I have to get back to the red barn. I live near there."

"Then why did you come all this way with me?" Emma asked.

"Friends help and stay by each other, even if it's only for a little while," Apple explained.

"Wow! Thank you, Apple," Emma said.

"Why did you call me Apple?" the girl asked, looking confused.

"Isn't that your name?" Emma asked. "The man at the barn said that no one should attempt these roads without Apple."

Apple smiled and explained, "You must have heard him wrong. He probably said that no one should attempt these roads without a pal. My name is Jane, not Apple, and I *am* your pal."

Chapter 6

A Surprise

The elevator door opened, and Jane hugged Emma. "We're friends, so even though we've only been together for a short time, I'll keep you in my heart," Jane said. "Maybe we'll meet again someday."

Emma stepped into the elevator, waving to Jane. The door closed, and as the elevator moved, it began to fade, and she was home.

Emma scratched her head, confused. *I must have fallen asleep and had a dream,* she thought. She was back in her living room, hearing voices coming from the kitchen.

Mom must have invited the new neighbors over, Emma thought. She was curious to see what they looked like. She went into the kitchen where a girl and a woman were talking with her mom. The girl had curly red hair and ankle bracelets.

"Apple!" Emma cried.

With a surprised look on her face, the girl asked, "How did you know my name? My name is Jane, but everyone calls me Apple because I love to eat apples."

"I guessed," Emma said, smiling brightly. "Something told me that a new friend was about to come along, and here you are."